Oh Victoria!
A Kid's Guide To Victoria, BC, Canada

Photography by John D. Weigand
Poetry by Penelope Dyan

Bellissima Publishing, LLC
Jamul, California
www.bellissimapublishing.com

Copyright © 2013 by Penny D. Weigand and John D. Weigand

All rights reserved. No part of this book may be reproduced or transmitted in any form or by any means, electronic or mechanical, including photocopying, recording, or by any other means, or by any information or storage retrieval system, without permission from the publisher.

ISBN 978-1-61477-108-1
First Edition

*When you have only two pennies
left in the world, buy a loaf of bread with one,
and a lily with the other.*

CHINESE PROVERB

Oh Victoria!
Bellissima Publishing, LLC

Introduction

Victoria is the capital city of British Columbia, Canada. The city was named after Queen Victoria of the United Kingdom, and is the 15th most populous city in British Columbia. It is one of the oldest cities in the Pacific Northwest, and British settlement began there in 1843. It is often referred to as the 'City of Gardens;' and when you see all the flowers and the colors of this place, it is easy to see why. This is a fun, metropolitan city full of art and music that has respect for its past,

See Victoria, British Columbia, Canada, through the lens of photographer John D. Weigand, and imagine its sounds, and especially its music, through the words and music of award winning author, attorney and former teacher, Penelope Dyan, as you read the words in this book and watch a free music video (titled the same as this book) on the Bellissimavideo YouTube Channel. Practice your reading skills through word recognition, repetition and rhyme and try to guess what is coming next. Most of all, have fun as you learn and use this book to travel along with Dyan and Weigand and see some of the things they saw when they went to this beautiful city.

Oh Victoria!
Bellissima Publishing, LLC

Oh Victoria!
A Kid's Guide To Victoria, BC, Canada

Photography by John D. Weigand
Poetry by Penelope Dyan

This is the famous Empress Hotel,
an historical landmark of Victoria,
that is known quite well.
Built between 1904 and 1908,
Its elegance and beauty
are NOT under debate.
King George VI and Queen Elizabeth
have stayed here,
as well others rich and famous,
year after year after year.

A chestnut horse dances
as it pulls a carriage down the street,
inviting you to hop aboard,
to save Mom's tired feet.

In Beacon Hill Park
you see bridge and a fountain flow;
and you decide this is one place,
to which you'll just HAVE to go!

A boat without sails
is anchored ready for the night,
as the sea beneath shimmers
in shadows and light.
Dark clouds dance
in the glimmering afternoon sun,
as the sky, earth and ocean,
all wait for day to be done.

Upon the Harbour Ferry
you can relax and float,
as you observe Victoria's sights,
from this green and yellow boat.

You can take a bus
or walk along the street,
where everything is oh so neat!

You can have your picture taken
with a Canadian Mounted Police bear.
He is already smiling,
and he WON'T really care.

There are shops where you can buy clothes, toys, souvenirs and things, even necklaces and bracelets and books and rings!

You can stop and see flowers that with fragrance fill the air. Victoria is 'The City of Gardens,' and you see flowers everywhere!

Then you see them on the shelf,
AND you would NOT have believed it,
had you not SEEN them yourself!
(Beaver and Moose droppings?)
You ask, "Can THIS be true?"
Your mother laughs and says, "Yes,"
and THEN she buys two!

And next to the water,
making music right there,
are two of the most talented musicians,
that you have heard anywhere!
They play the accordion, fiddle and sing;
and you wonder if they realize
the great happiness they bring.

Finally, as with your mom and dad
you walk slowly by...
you see a golden building outlined
against the royal blue sky.
It's almost time for dinner,
and soon it will be time for bed.
And upon a soft pillow you will
rest your weary head.
Then you will hug your mom and dad,
and you will kiss them both good night;
because, after all, you love them,
and it is oh so very right.

"Silently, one by one, in the infinite
meadows of heaven,
Blossomed the lovely stars,
the forget-me-nots of the angels."

Henry Wadsworth Longfellow,
Evangeline: A Tale of Acadie

www.ingramcontent.com/pod-product-compliance
Ingram Content Group UK Ltd.
Pitfield, Milton Keynes, MK11 3LW, UK
UKHW060134240426
12048UKWH00002B/32